SUNFLOWERS

SUNFLOWERS

MARY ANN McDONALD

THE CHILD'S WORLD®, INC.

Photo Credits
Joe McDonald: 10, 15, 16, 19, 20, 26, 29, 30
Mary Ann McDonald: cover, 13
John R. Patton: 2, 6, 9, 23, 24

Printed in the United States of America.

Library of Congress Cataloging-in-Publication Data
McDonald, Mary Ann,
Sunflowers / written by Mary Ann McDonald.
p.   cm.
Includes index.
Summary: Describes the physical characteristics,
origins, and uses of the sunflower.
ISBN 1-56766-272-2 (library bound hadcover)
1. Sunflowers—Juvenile literature. [1. Sunflowers.]
I. Title.
QK495.C74M38   1996
583'.55—dc20   96-1871
                                      CIP
                                      AC

TABLE OF CONTENTS

It's Labor Day weekend and you're going to Grandma's for a picnic. As you turn into her driveway, you see a splash of bright yellow in her garden. You run to the garden and look up at giant plants with huge yellow flowers. The plants are taller than your dad! Flower heads, the size of dinner plates, look down at you. Are these the giant beanstalks that Jack climbed? No, they're just sunflowers that grandma planted to feed the birds.

People plant sunflowers around their homes for the birds to enjoy.

HOW DID SUNFLOWERS GET THEIR NAME?

Botanists (people who study plants) call sunflowers *Helianthus* (hee-lee-AN-thus). This name is made from two separate words; *helios* (HEE-lee-ose), which means sun, and *anthos* (AN-thoce), which means flower. Sunflowers got their name because they look like the sun and because they face the sun while they are growing. In the morning, a sunflower faces east to meet the rising sun. By afternoon, it faces west toward the setting sun. The French word for sunflower is *tournesol* (TURN-i-so) which means "turn with the sun."

Sunflower heads follow the sun throughout the day.

The head of the sunflower is made of two different kinds of flowers. The center is made of hundreds of very small flowers called *disk flowers*. These small flowers produce **nectar** and **pollen**. The yellow **petals** surrounding the center are called ray flowers. The bright color attracts bees and other insects that help to **pollinate** the disk flowers. One sunflower seed grows from every disk flower that is pollinated.

The center of the sunflower is made of disk flowers.

WHERE DID SUNFLOWERS COME FROM?

There are over 150 **species**, or different kinds, of sunflowers growing in the wild. They grow anywhere from grassy plains to sandy woodlands. Sunflowers have their **origin**, or beginning, in the New World. South America, Central America, and North America are all part of the New World. The Old World includes Europe, Asia, and Africa. No sunflowers grew in the Old World until people brought them there.

There are many different kinds of sunflowers.

HOW DID NATIVE AMERICANS USE SUNFLOWERS?

The sunflower was a very important food item to many Native Americans. Some sunflower seeds were dried in the sun and eaten as a snack, just like we eat them today. Other seeds were dried, then ground between two stones and made into a coarse flour. This flour was mixed with water to make a stew. Native Americans of the Great Plains mixed the flour with buffalo fat and baked small cakes. These cakes were eaten by warriors and hunters on long trips to give them energy.

Native Americans ground sunflower seeds, like these, into flour.

Every part of the sunflower plant was used by Native Americans. The fuzzy stalks and leaves were used to make yellow dyes. The seeds made black and purple dyes that were used for clothing and baskets. The seed heads were boiled to make oil that was used to grease hair. The roots were eaten either raw or cooked. They were also used in making healthful teas and ointments. Navajos even made crude flutes from the sunflower's stalks.

Every part of the sunflower was used by Native Americans.

WHO BROUGHT SUNFLOWERS TO THE OLD WORLD?

In the early 1500s, Spanish explorers carried sunflower seeds back to Europe. Soon, the flowers spread throughout Europe and into Russia. They were grown first for their beauty. France's King Louis XIV used the sunflower as the symbol of his rule.

In Europe, sunflowers were grown for their beauty.

Here in the United States, the pioneers learned from the Native Americans. They used the sunflower stalks for animal food and to start fires. They made cloth from its coarse fibers. And they made oil from its seeds. Before potatoes were brought to the United States from South America, Native Americans and settlers alike ate a special kind of sunflower, called the *Jerusalem artichoke*.

Pioneers used sunflowers for many purposes.

HOW ARE SUNFLOWERS USED TODAY?

Today, the sunflower is an important crop in many parts of the world. In Europe, people eat sunflowers as snacks. They also smoke the leaves, use the flower buds in salads, and use the oil for cooking. In Asia, sunflower oil is used for canning fish and for burning in lamps, and the plant fibers are used in making paper.

The sunflower is an important crop around the world.

Russia has the largest amount of land planted in sunflowers in the world. Cooking oil is one of the main products from these sunflowers. Oil-cakes, the leftover seed parts from making the oil, are an important food for livestock. Russians make a very strong rubbing oil from sunflowers and use it as medicine. It is easy to see why the sunflower is the national flower of Russia.

Sunflowers, like these in Pennsylvania, are the largest crop in Russia.

Sunflowers are also grown here in the United States. There are two different kinds that are grown for their seeds. The gray-striped seeds are called *confection seeds*. These seeds are grown for food. Each seed kernel is rich in vitamins, iron, and protein. And they are cholesterol free, too! The smaller black seeds are called *oilseeds*. Sunflower oil comes from this kind of seed. This oil is used in margarine, salad dressings, and sometimes even in diesel fuel!

Sunflower oil comes from oilseeds, one type of sunflower seed.

DO ANIMALS EAT SUNFLOWER SEEDS?

In nature, the sunflower is an important food for many different animals. Grouse, pheasants, quail, and many songbirds depend on the seeds as a major part of their diet. Deer, moose, and even muskrats will eat different parts of the plant. The roots are eaten by such animals as ground-hogs and prairie dogs.

Cardinals love to eat sunflowers.

HOW CAN YOU ENJOY SUNFLOWERS?

Sunflowers are easy to grow! Plant some seeds in May or early June. In August and September, watch the bees come to the flowers and become heavy with pollen. And then watch the birds eat the seeds in September and October. Sunflowers are good for everyone. Plant some sunflowers and have fun!

Bees are attracted to the sunflower by the bright yellow color.

GLOSSARY

botanists (BOTT-un-ists)
People who study plants. The science of studying plants is called botany (BOTT-un-ee).

species (SPEE-sheez)
A separate kind of plant or animal. There are over 150 different species of sunflowers.

nectar (NECK-ter)
The sweet liquid made by plants. The small flowers at the center of a sunflowers produce nectar.

pollen (POL-in)
Seeds on plants that look like dust. The small flowers at the center of sunflowers produce pollen.

pollinate(POL-i-nate)
To carry pollen from one flower to another. Insects help to pollinate flowers.

petals (PET-els)
The often brightly colored leaves of a flower. Sunflowers have yellow petals at their center.

origin (OR-i-gin)
The point at which something begins. Sunflowers have their origin in the New World.

INDEX